GUSTAV KLIMT

ALICE STROBL

GUSTAV KLIMT
DRAWINGS AND PAINTINGS

VERLAG GALERIE WELZ SALZBURG

Translated from the German by Inga Hamilton

The publishers thank the director of the Albertina, Vienna, Dr. Walter Koschatzky, and the other lenders for the kind loan of the originals for reproduction.

Printed in Austria by Color-Druck, Kindberg

Gustav Klimt was the great pioneer of modern painting in Austria and one of the most important draughtsmen of his epoch. Even in his life-time his work met with enthusiastic appreciation, not only in his own country but also in exhibitions abroad, in Paris, Rome and Venice. There were many people, however, who decidedly rejected Gustav Klimt's ornamental-decorative painting, a fact to be accounted for not only by a lack of understanding but also by the rise of new artistic trends which were hostile to ornament. On the other hand, the artist's graphic œuvre, which extends to several thousand sheets, aroused much less opposition. His drawings were accepted without reservation and their mastery acknowledged to be independent of period.

A new attitude to Gustav Klimt's painting has been created by ornamental-decorative features in today's art. This was proved by the international success of the retrospective exhibition of his works at the Biennale in Venice in 1958. Research has also led to new findings with regard to his drawings. It has been possible to identify many of them as preliminary studies for paintings and in this way a basis has been provided for a chronological arrangement of the drawings. This chronological arrangement has brought out clearly the way the artist's style of drawing changed and the great range of his powers of expression, extending from the most sparing suggestions of a form to its elaboration into a full composition.

Gustav Klimt's great talent for drawing was already evident during his seven years of study at the Vienna School of Arts and Crafts. The work on the ceiling paintings above the great staircases at each side of the Burgtheater in Vienna for which Klimt, together with his brother Ernst and with Franz Matsch, was responsible, forced him to come to terms with the problems of monumental painting, a process of thought that was important for him. His solution to these problems, deriving as it did from his studies under Laufberger and following Makart's lead, was traditional. Klimt's originality appears, however, in the repression of movement and of the grand manner and also in the sensitive understanding of the subject, in the gradation of expression and the refined perception of the figures. These differences are clearly seen in his drawing also, for example in the studies for the ceiling paintings in the Vienna Burgtheater. The drawing "Juliet on her Bier", a study for a detail for "Shakespear's Theatre" (Plate 1) offers an example of the artist's early style of drawing. By means of fine hatching and a sparing use of white high-lighting he makes the pale face stand out in relief from the hair, which is shaded in in chalk, while he suggests the upper part of the body with only a few strokes, which nevertheless possess already something of the power of illusion of his later drawings.

It was only in the six years following the death of his brother Ernst (1892) that a decisive change took place in Klimt's artistic production and that his personal style asserted itself. At international exhibitions which had been organized by the Künstlergemeinschaft (Artist's Association) from the beginning of the nineties onwards Klimt made the acquaintance of the French Impressionist, Neoimpressionist and Symbolist painting. He was also brought into contact with the art of the Pre-Raphaelites and Whistler, as well as with the work of the Belgian Khnopff, the Dutchman Toorop and the representatives of the German Jugendstil. Thus stimulated, he developed a specifically Austrian form of the Jugendstil and in order to protagonize this style of art in a suitable manner he joined with like-minded men, chiefly architects, in the "Secession", an association of artists founded in 1897. Their mouthpiece was the periodical "Ver Sacrum" (Sacred Spring), to which Klimt made numerous contributions. Among these are two fair drawings specially done for printing, which he contributed to the March issue of the first year (1898). In "Nuda Veritas" and "Envy" (Plate 2) the mode of expression of the Jugendstil, the contour in swinging curves, the rhythmic division into dark and light areas and the employment of flickering patterns, is fully developed. The sketches for these two works, like the drawing "Girl in Armchair" (Plate 8) have thick parallel layers of hatching which are worked into each other.

In the ceiling paintings for the Vienna University Klimt tried

6

to transfer this style to monumental painting. The pictures for the faculties, "Philosophy", "Medicine" and "Jurisprudence", were commissioned from him by the Ministry of Education in 1894. He had worked out the preliminary painted sketches still in the Impressionist manner, but the first versions of "Philosophy" and "Medicine", which were exhibited in the Secession in 1900 and 1901, already displayed the new style and the attempt at a modern type of monumental painting. Rejected by the board of professors, the faculty pictures never reached their intended destination. The artist bought them back; later they passed into private, then into public, possession and were destroyed in 1945. It is all the more important, therefore, that a large number of preparatory drawings have been preserved, among them the composition sketches. That of "Medicine", like the actual picture, comprehends almost the whole range of the themes found in Klimt's works and its subject is the growth and decay of the human being (Plate 5). The different ages, hope, love, ecstasy, procreation, and motherhood, struggle, despair, illness and death, are ranged one above the other in a vertical ribbon-composition representing one section of an ever-recurring process. In the middle of the drawing the dominating figure of Hygieia towers up from the lower edge, while on the left side, as a symbol of the continuance of the human race, there appears a female figure suspended in the air. The artist devoted many studies to this figure and the reproduced drawing (Plate 6) represents the final phase of this process of artistic development. The Jugendstil is here revealed at its peak. In contrast, the study for "Hygieia" (Plate 3) with the robe drawn in a style of parallel folds, stands in much closer relationship to the 1898 drawing of "Envy" (Plate 2). In the composition sketch this influence has already retired into the background in favour of the unified form which gives the figure a more monumental effect (Plate 5). This feature is even clearer in the oil painting. The artist has painted "Hygieia's" robe (Plate 56) with rich gold ornamentation on a red ground, used the snake as a decorative element, and established a link between the body and the projecting head decked with red

7

ribbons in order to give the contour still further unity. In contrast to these elements, which emphasize a flat surface, Klimt has given "Hygieia's" head and arms relief in the same way as he has all the nude figures in the picture and he has made the background on the left side appear to be without substance. These different gradations of stylisation, an attractive feature which the artist has deliberately aimed at, characterize not only "Medicine" but are also to be found in the other great compositions of his maturity.

While he was still working on the pictures for the faculties Klimt produced a second important piece of monumental painting when Max Klinger's statue of Beethoven was exhibited in the Secession in the spring of 1902. This was the "Beethoven Frieze", which he composed as a free pictorial interpretation of Beethoven's 9th Symphony. Among the sketches for this work there are not only drawings which carry further the style of the studies für "Medicine", for example, "The Kiss" (Plate 10) or the drawing with the demonic heads (Plate 11), but also some which portray lengthened figures with a bony structure and a mannered attitude and which are mostly done in hard chalk (Plate 15). The expressive sculptures of George Minne, which had been exhibited the previous year, seem to have exerted a certain influence. The interior drawing has almost completely disappeared; in some cases the relief of the body is indicated by repetition of the outline. The unbroken line ist dominant. The portrait of Emilie Flöge of 1902 (Plate 57) displays this strictly linear style in painting. The slenderness of the model is exaggerated by the tall narrow format common with Klimt. The dress, painted with vertical wavy lines, and with spiral and circle motifs in blue, green, pink, gold and silver, and the capricious hat, which are treated as ornamental flat areas, serve at the same time as bearers of the expression of the subject's individuality.

The study for one of the Erinyes (Plate 13) of the third faculty picture, "Jurisprudence", is filled with the same line-dynamic as the hovering figure in "Medicine". Together with the probably contemporary drawings for the portrait of Adele Bloch-Bauer (which was not painted, however, until 1907) this belongs to the most significant of the drawings created by Klimt in the Jugendstil. The sketches for this portrait, with their curvilinear ripple of folds of charming musicality, remind one of drawings by Pisanello (Plates 16 and 17). In the drawings "Girl sitting with bowed head" (Plate 14) and "Girl lying to the right" (Plate 18), of which the one may date from about 1904 and the other two years later, the artist put his whole energy into the unbroken outline. The picture "Water Serpents I", in which the whole composition is dominated by the rhythmical swing (Plate 59), painted in small format on parchment about the year 1904, has a similar style to that of the "Girl with bowed head". All the forms seem to lie one above the other in thin layers and to move in a dreamlike sphere. The relief of the bodies almost completely disappears. A special accent is placed on the great curve of the girl's body and it gains a still more delicate, more lengthened effect through the covering of the right hip with a greenish veil. In a picture which is related in theme and which was painted at the same time but revised in 1907, "Water Serpents II" (Plate 60) the plasticity of the women's bodies is emphasized and the decorative element is increased by the use of the millefiori-pattern. The figure in the foreground has its origin in an allegory of Vice by Franz Stuck which was reproduced in "Ver Sacrum" in 1902.

The most complete stylisation in the direction of geometrical form appears in the working drawings made between 1905 and 1909 for the mosaic frieze of the dining-room of the Palais Stoclet in Brussels. The Palais Stoclet was built by Josef Hoffmann with the cooperation of various artists of the "Wiener Werkstätte". The designs, done on paper in chalk, pencil, tempera and water-colours, opaque white, gold- and silver-bronze and also gold- and silver-leaf, show trees of life with the figural compositions, "Expectation" and "Fulfilment" (Plates 61 and 62). In "Expectation" the ornament, dominated by the triangle both in the main form and in detail, is linked with the tendril motif of the background, which is an endless repetitive pattern. Arms and hands, but not the head submit to the same principle of stylisation. One of the preparatory studies for this design (Plate 20) strikes one as closer to nature, but the vertical delimiting of the left side of the body, the left knee pushed forward and the position of the right arm give a hint of development to a geometrical modelling. In "Fulfilment", too, the large unified form in which the two figures are gathered into a unity is dominant, although the contrast between the male and female is made discernible by contour and ornamentation (Plate 62). The artist used many-coloured flowers in the composition of the picture, both as a symbolic and a decorative element. These flowers are to be found also in his contemporary landscapes and flower pictures, in which an individual flower often towers up in large form like a human figure yet blends like a mosaic with the flowers and grass of the meadow, as in the painting "The Sunflower" (Plate 63).

The development of Gustav Klimt's style of drawing during the years from 1904 till 1908 can be clearly followed in a series of drawings which were produced at the same time as those in Franz Blei's translation of Lucian's "Hetaira Conversations", which was published at Leipzig in 1907. In this period the artist laid particular stress on the arrangement of the figure on the page. The areas free of drawing now became an element of the composition as is most clearly seen in the drawing of a "Nude girl with ruche", which is pushed to the upper edge of the page (Plate 19). In another drawing, the lady represented standing front view forms the centre (Plate 23). In these studies it is noticeable that the lines are no longer continuous but recommence several times and have curls at some points. While the swinging guidance of the line is retained, there are angular, jutting contours. A multitude of small shapes, rings and circles and zig-zag lines, suggests the ornament in a short-hand manner (Plate 22). By a concentration of strokes outside the outlines, the relief of many parts of the body is especially emphasized (Plates 24, 25). In these drawings, which are often done in red and blue crayon on shimmering paper similar to Japanese, Gustav Klimt's ornamental-decorative style reaches its climax in the years 1907—1908 just as it does in the paintings, the colours of which appear like mosaic out of a background of gold and silver. The most important works of this period, the so-called rich style, are the portrait of Adele Bloch-Bauer, seated (Plate 64) and "The Kiss" (Plate 66). In these paintings there are large areas with sweeping outlines and geometric patterns out of which the shimmering flesh-tints appear as if in relief and in opalescent tones. Even for the attitude of the body, and in particular that of the arms and the expressive hands, his stylised principle was decisive. Klimt's love of ornamentation is also expressed in the use of gold, both shining and mat, and in the most varying nuances of colour. Already in 1908 this phase was followed by a reaction which, however, proved to be only a transitionary stage. Powerfully expressive drawings appeared, in which the artist represented people bowed by suffering. The sketch of a man's head in vanishing profile (Plate 30) may perhaps be ascribed already to this transition period. The structure of the face is worked out by means of a thick, nervous structure of lines in which a coarsening of the stroke to intensify the expression is felt. Similar features characterize also the portrait of the artist's mother (Plate 31) and the portrait drawing of an old woman seated (Plate 28). By means of thick lines the facial features are made to stand out sharply while the sitting position has been suggested as economically as possible by the outline of the dress alone.

Dark colours characterize the oil-paintings of this expressive phase of style, such as "The Family" or the portrait, also done in 1910, of a young lady with feather hat (Plate 67). Ornament, as well as the use of gold and silver, has completely disappeared from this composition. On the other hand a loosening of the structure of the painting can be observed, which also remains a determining factor for the late work. With these works Gustav Klimt stood on the threshold of Expressionism. They were of great importance for the early development of Egon Schiele's art.

In the oil paintings of the artist's final creative period the intensity, luminous power and differentiation of colours is a new element which becomes noticeable and which is of course unthinkable without the influence of contemporary French painting.

The portrait of Baroness Bachofen Echt (Plate 70), which was painted about 1912, displays the new wealth of colour. Complementary colours and colours closely related are juxtaposed and we find delicate pink, blue and yellow tones on a white ground. Simultaneously with this organizing of the paint, the line becomes prominent as a formative element, especially in the dress and hands of the subject. The figure itself is almost front view and is bound into the composition by the gaily ornamented triangle on the wall. The Chinese vase-figures peopling the background are painted in movement towards the subject yet are kept at a distance from her by a strip which remains clear.

Likewise in the standing portrait of Adele Bloch-Bauer of 1912 (Plate 69), many studies for which survive, Klimt restricted ornament to the background. In the drawing here reproduced (Plate 32) even the personality of this woman is suggested. By the placing of short diagonal strokes a glitter and vibration is produced on the surface of the paper. This can also be noticed in some of his female nudes, such as the study for one of the girls in the picture "The Maiden" (1913) or in a standing nude girl (Plates 36 and 38). In these drawings the physical seems to be spiritualized and the erotic-ecstatic, the representation of which has great importance in Klimt's work, seems to belong to a higher sphere. In the oil "The Maiden" (Plate 71) the artist has massed the girls' bodies together into an oval composition on a dark ground from which they seem to project like a relief, only to be forced back by the all-over design on the dress of the dominating central figure. Thus in this picture also, a tension is created between plastic representation and the stressing of areas.

To the last years of Klimt's life belongs a series of drawings characterised by a balance of classical greatness. The female nude still forms the main theme of these studies. In the drawings reproduced here (Plates 40, 44, 48) the artist surrounded the bodies with an outline consisting of many strokes but appearing continous and this stresses the curvilinear swing and brings out the plastic values. This outline found its way into the oil-paintings as a broad brush-stroke. Perhaps a comparison of the standing female nude front view (Plate 51), a monumentally conceived drawing, with the representation of Eve for the picture "Adam and Eve", which was begun in 1917 but not completed (Plate 74), shows this change most clearly. But at the same time it throws light on the artist's technique. To judge from this picture, Klimt must have transferred the figure of Eve life-size onto the painting surface, with crayon, going over the contour with blue paint and then painting the finely differentiated flesh tones. In this way he arrived at a harmony of drawing and painting qualities in the oil-paintings of his late creative period (Plates 73 and 75).

The individuality of the graphic works created by Klimt in the last two years of his life (1916—18) lies in the fact that the curls and frills with their rhythmic swings are used to build-up the whole figure and make it appear three-dimensional in the intended space (Plates 52, 54, 55). Interior and outline drawing are inseparably linked with one another and, through the varying intensity of the stroke, become bearers of colour values. With these sheets the plastic organisation of the painting, which was decisive for the last phase of Gustav Klimt's work, reaches its climax. Looking back over the artist's graphic œuvre, however, we see that he produced drawings in each of his various periods which rank him among the great masters. As a painter he brought a style, the Jugendstil, to perfection and prepared the way for modern art in Austria.

PRINCIPAL DATES

1862 Born 14th July, at Baumgarten near Vienna, son of an engraver from Bohemia.

1876—1883 Study at the State School of Arts and Crafts (Kunstgewerbeschule) in Vienna under Professors Ferdinand Laufberger and Julius Viktor Berger.

1886—1888 Ceiling paintings in the great side-staircases of the Burgtheater, with his brother Ernst and Franz Matsch.

1888—1889 Journey to Cracow, Trieste, Venice, Munich etc.

1890—1892 Spaces between the ribs of vaulting and intercolumnar areas of the great staircase of the Kunsthistorisches Museum in Vienna.

1891 Member of the Artists' Guild (Genossenschaft bildender Künstler).

1892 Death of his brother Ernst.

1897 Founding of the Secession and nomination as first president.

1898 First exhibition of the Secession.

1900 Participates at World Exhibition Paris and is awarded the Gold Medal for foreigners.
"Philosophy" exhibited in the Secession.

1901 Exhibition of "Medicine" in the Secession.

1902 "Beethoven Frieze" for the left side-gallery of the Secession (Spring Exhibition).

1903 Collective exhibition of eighty works in the Secession.

1905 Leaves the Secession.
Start of sketches for the Palais Stoclet, Brussels (finished 1911)

1906 Journey to Belgium and England.

1908 Journey to Florence.
Exhibition "Kunstschau Vienna".

1909 Exhibition "Internationale Kunstschau Vienna".
Journey to Paris and Madrid.

1910 Enthusiastic reception of his works at the Biennale in Venice.

1911 International Exhibition in Rome.
Journey to Rome and Florence.

1914 Journey to Brussels. Exhibition of the "Bund Österreichischer Künstler" in Rome.

1917 Honorary member of the Academy of Fine Arts in Vienna, after ministerial refusal of his appointment as professor at this institute. Honorary member of the Academy of Fine Arts in Munich.

1918 On the 11th of January Klimt had a stroke and died on the 6th of February in Vienna.

1

WAHRHEIT
IST FEUER UND
WAHRHEIT
REDEN HEISST
LEUCHTEN UND
BRENNEN .

L · SCHEFER ·

NUDA
VERITAS

GVSTAV · KLIMT ·

N

DER NEID

GVSTAV
KLIMT ·

2

3

4

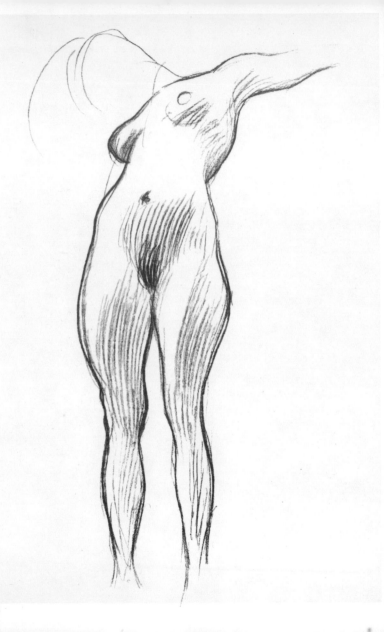

9

GVSTAV
KLIMT
NACHLASS

12

GVSTAV
KLIMT
NACHLASS

Nachlass meines lieben Gustav
Serena Klimt

17

GVSTAV
KLIMT

GUSTAV
KLIMT
NACHLASS

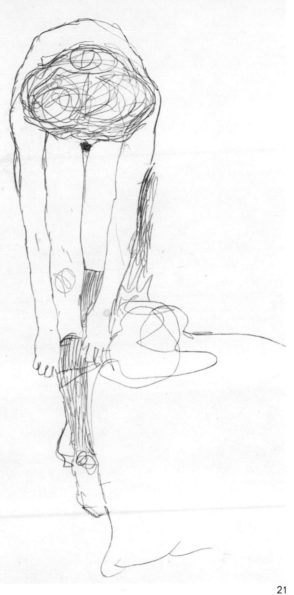

GVSTAV
KLIMT
NACHLASS

GVSTAV
KLIMT
NACHLASS

23

24

GVSTAV
KLIMT

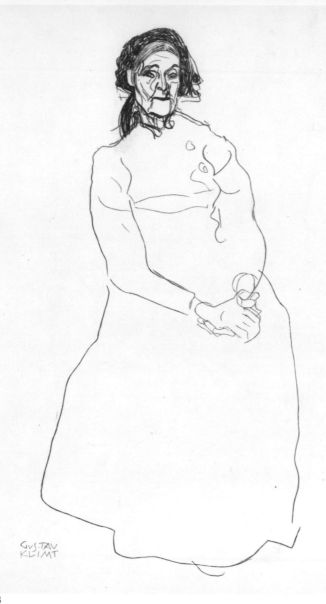

GVSTAV
KLIMT

GVSTAV
KLIMT

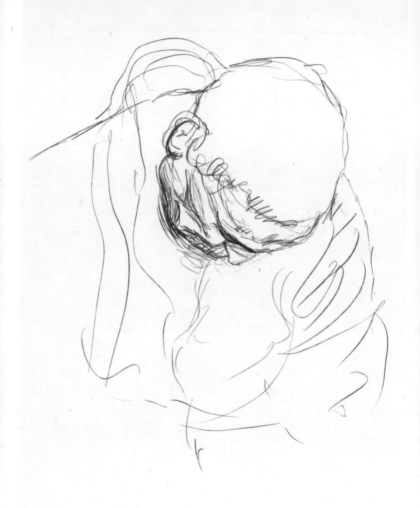

35

GVSTAV
KLIMT
NACHLASS

37

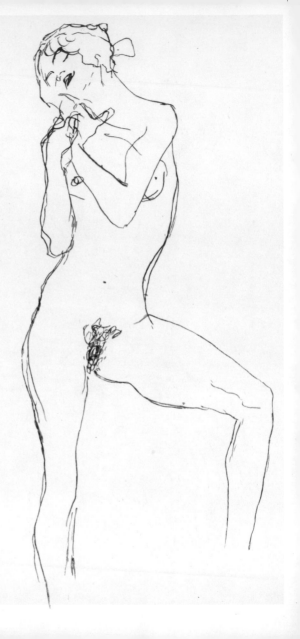

38

GUSTAV
KLIMT

GVSTAV
KLIMT

40

GVSTAV
KLIMT

41

GVSTAV
KLIMT
NACHLASS

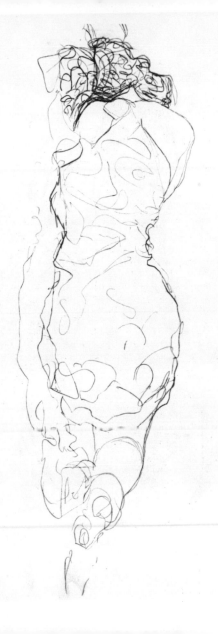

46

47

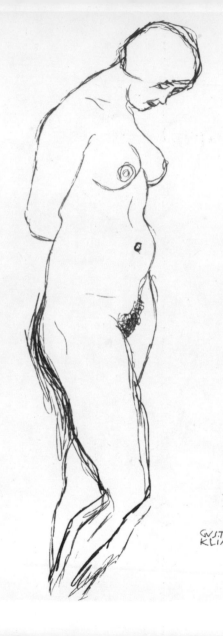

GVSTAV
KLIMT

48

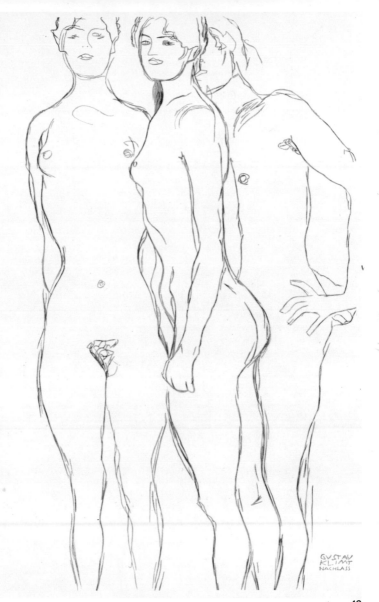

GVSTAV
KLIMT
NACHLASS

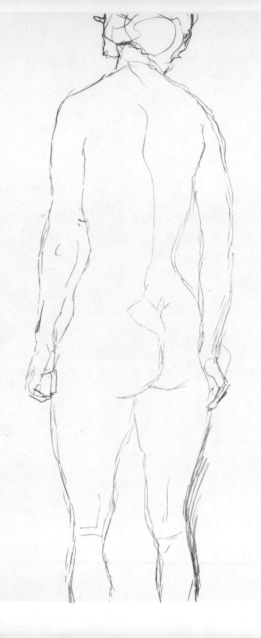

GUSTAV
KLIMT
NACHLASS

50

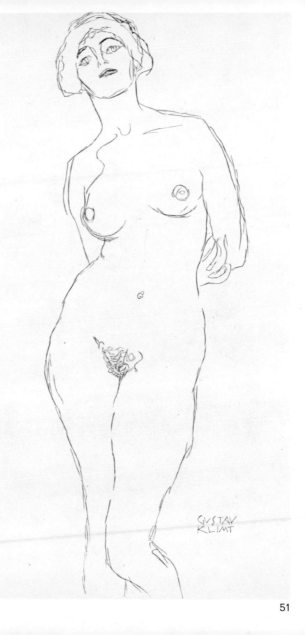

GUSTAV
KLIMT
NACHLASS

GUSTAV
KLIMT

61

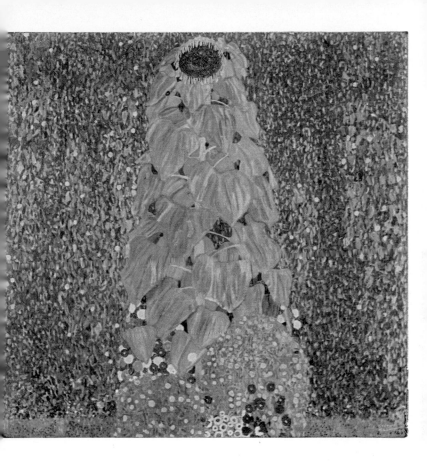

GVSTAV
KLIMT
19 10

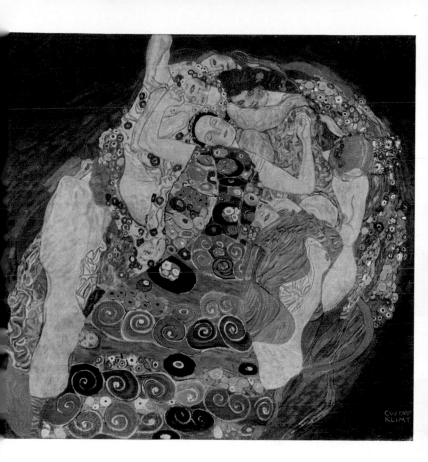

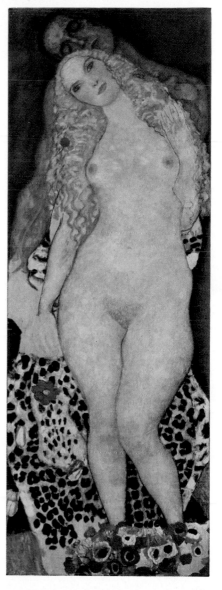

74

DRAWINGS

1 STUDY FOR "JULIET ON HER BIER" FOR THE CEILING PAINTING, "SHAKESPEARE'S THEATRE", IN THE RIGHT STAIRCASE OF THE VIENNA BURGTHEATER (1886 to 1888). Chalk, white highlights. Signed. 276 mm × 424 mm. Albertina, Cat. No. 27,930.

2 NUDA VERITAS. Pencil, pen with Indian ink, squared up. Signed. 413 mm × 104 mm. Historical Museum of the City of Vienna, Cat. No. 101,718. Fair drawing for the March issue of Ver Sacrum 1898, pg. 12.
ENVY. Chalk, pen and brush in Indian ink. Signed. 415 mm × 98 mm. Historical Museum of the City of Vienna, Cat. No. 101,719. Fair drawing for the March issue of Ver Sacrum 1898, pg. 12.

3 STUDY FOR HYGIEIA FOR THE OIL-PAINTING "MEDICINE". Black chalk. Signed. 446 mm × 312 mm. Albertina, Cat. No. 31,459.

4 COMPOSITION SKETCH FOR "PHILOSOPHY" (1900). Black chalk, pencil. Enlarging grid. 896 mm × 632 mm. Historical Museum of the City of Vienna, Cat. No. 71,506.

5 COMPOSITION SKETCH FOR "MEDICINE" (1901). Black chalk, pencil. Enlarging grid. 860 mm × 620 mm. Albertina, Cat. No. 29,545.

6 STUDY FOR THE SUSPENDED FEMALE FIGURE FOR THE OIL-PAINTING "MEDICINE". Chalk. 415 mm × 273 mm. Albertina, Cat. No. 23,664.

7 STANDING COUPLE. STUDY FOR THE PAINTING "HOPE" (1902), ORIGINAL CONCEPT FOR THIS PAINTING. Red crayon. 450 mm × 305 mm. Galerie Welz Salzburg.

8 GIRL IN ARMCHAIR. Chalk, white highlights. 449 mm by 306 mm. Otto Schönthal, Vienna.

9 STUDY FOR THE PORTRAIT OF ROSE FRIEDMANN-

ROSTHORN (about 1901). Charcoal and pencil. 450 mm by 320 mm. Galerie Welz Salzburg.

10 THE KISS. STUDY FOR THE "BEETHOVEN FRIEZE" (1902). Chalk. 447 mm×316 mm. Stamp of the artist's estate. Dr. R. Leopold, Vienna.

11 STUDY OF HEAD FOR THE "BEETHOVEN FRIEZE". Black chalk. Signed. 435 mm×310 mm. Historical Museum of the City of Vienna, Cat. No. 96,032.

12 LAWYER. STUDY FOR THE OIL-PAINTING "JURISPRU-DENCE" (1903). Black chalk. 444 mm×308 mm. Historical Museum of the City of Vienna, Cat. No. 96,482/14.

13 WOMAN'S HEAD. STUDY FOR THE OIL-PAINTING "JURIS-PRUDENCE". Black chalk. 396 mm×298 mm. Albertina, Cat. No. 23,667.

14 GIRL SITTING WITH BOWED HEAD. Pencil. 566 mm by 372 mm. Stamp of the artist's estate. Dr. R. Leopold, Vienna.

15 FEMALE NUDE STANDING TO LEFT. STUDY FOR THE "BEETHOVEN FRIEZE". Chalk. 440 mm×300 mm. Albertina, Cat. No. 22,494.

16 STUDY FOR THE PORTRAIT OF ADELE BLOCH-BAUER (1907) IN THE AUSTRIAN GALLERY. Black chalk. 458 mm by 310 mm. Albertina, Cat. No. 30,704. Drawn about 1903.

17 STUDY OF DRESS FOR THE PORTRAIT OF ADELE BLOCH-BAUER (1907) IN THE AUSTRIAN GALLERY. Black chalk. 549 mm×346 mm. Albertina, Cat. No. 30,700.

18 FEMALE NUDE LYING TO RIGHT. Pencil. 373 mm by 565 mm. Dr. R. Leopold, Vienna.

19 FEMALE NUDE LYING TO RIGHT WITH RUCHE. Pencil, red crayon. Signed. 558 mm×370 mm. Dr. R. Leopold, Vienna.

20 GIRL STANDING FACING RIGHT. STUDY FOR "EXPEC-TATION" FOR THE MOSAIC FRIEZE FOR THE DINING-ROOM OF THE PALAIS STOCLET IN BRUSSELS (1905—1911). Pencil. 556 mm×370 mm. Stamp of the artist's estate. Dr. R. Leopold, Vienna.

21   GIRL PUTTING ON STOCKING. Pencil. 552 mm×343 mm. Dr. R. Leopold, Vienna.

22   LADY STANDING FACING RIGHT. STUDY FOR THE POR-TRAIT OF MARGARET WITTGENSTEIN-STONBOROUGH (1905) IN THE NEW STATE GALLERY, MUNICH. Black chalk. 550 mm×349 mm. Stamp of the artist's estate. Dr. R. Leopold, Vienna.

23   LADY STANDING FRONT VIEW. Pencil. 560 mm×370 mm. Galerie Würthle, Vienna.

24   LADY STANDING FRONT VIEW. ON THE RIGHT REPETI-TION OF THE HEAD. Pencil. 560 mm×370 mm. Historical Museum of the City of Vienna, Cat. No. 74,930/81.

25   STANDING LADY READING, FACING LEFT. Pencil. Signed. 558 mm×368 mm. Albertina, Cat. No. 23,541.

26   WOMAN UNDRESSING, PROFILE LOOKING RIGHT. Pencil. 560 mm×370 mm. Signed. Tony Curtis, USA.

27   FRONTAL VIEW OF SITTING NUDE. Blue crayon. 560 mm by 370 mm. Stamp of the artist's estate. Galerie Welz Salzburg.

28   OLD WOMAN SITTING FRONT VIEW. Charcoal. Signed. 550 mm×352 mm. Albertina, Cat. No. 23,536.

29   WOMAN IN PATTERNED DRESS. Pencil, red and blue crayon, white highlights. Signed. 560 mm×370 mm. Dr. H. B. Munich.

30   MAN'S BOWED HEAD. STUDY FOR THE OIL-PAINTING "DEATH AND LIFE" (1908—1916). Pencil. 559 mm×367 mm. Albertina, Cat. No. 29,737.

31   STUDY OF THE HEAD OF THE ARTIST'S MOTHER. Pencil. 566 mm×374 mm. Albertina, Cat. No. 32,944.

32   STUDY FOR THE PORTRAIT OF ADELE BLOCH-BAUER (1912) IN THE AUSTRIAN GALLERY. Pencil. 550 mm by 290 mm. Albertina, Cat. No. 23,542.

33 GIRL SITTING FRONT VIEW. MÄDA PRIMAVESI (1913). Pencil. 566 mm×368 mm. Albertina, Cat. No. 30,445.

34 STUDY FOR THE PORTRAIT OF MRS. PULITZER (Serena Lederer's mother), about 1916. Pencil, 500 mm×325 mm. In private possession, Graz.

35 STUDY FOR THE PORTRAIT OF MÄDA PRIMAVESI (1913). Pencil. 560 mm×370 mm. In private possession, Graz.

36 GIRL KNEELING. STUDY FOR THE OIL-PAINTING "THE MAIDEN" (1913). MODERN GALLERY, PRAGUE. Pencil. Signed. 558 mm×367 mm. Dr. R. Leopold, Vienna.

37 HALF-NUDE LYING TO LEFT. Pencil, pen in Indian ink, red crayon. 560 mm×370 mm. Stamp of the artist's estate. In private possession, Vienna.

38 NUDE GIRL STANDING. Pencil. 565 mm×372 mm. Stamp of the artist's estate. Dr. R. Leopold, Vienna.

39 GIRL IN RUCHED DRESS IN FRONT VIEW. Pencil. Signed. 558 mm×368 mm. Albertina, Cat. No. 23,529.

40 FEMALE NUDE SITTING IN BACK VIEW. Pencil. Signed. 565 mm×368 mm. Albertina, Cat. No. 23,532.

41 NUDE GIRL WITH LEFT ARM HIDING FACE. Pencil. Signed. 564 mm×363 mm. Albertina, Cat. No. 23,538.

42 LADY SITTING FRONT VIEW. FRITZI BEER. STUDY OF POSE. Pencil. 569 mm×374 mm. Dr. R. Leopold, Vienna.

43 STUDY OF A PORTRAIT (probably the portrait of Fritzi Beer, 1916). Pencil. 570 mm×370 mm. Galerie Welz Salzburg.

44 NUDE CROUCHING TO RIGHT. Probably study for the oil-painting "Leda" (1917—1918). Pencil. 565 mm×373 mm. Stamp of the artist's estate. Dr. R. Leopold, Vienna.

45 WOMAN LYING TO LEFT, BACK TURNED TO VIEWER. Pencil. 348 mm×567 mm. Albertina, Cat. No. 23,540.

46 FEMALE CROUCHING TO RIGHT. STUDY FOR THE OIL-PAINTING "LEDA". Pencil. 369 mm×550 mm. Stamp of the artist's estate. Dr. R. Leopold, Vienna.

47 FEMALE PORTRAIT WITH UNCOVERED BREASTS. Pencil. 565 mm×370 mm. In private possession, Vienna.

48 STANDING FEMALE NUDE FACING RIGHT. Pencil. Signed. 568 mm×373 mm. Albertina, Cat. No. 23,528.

49 THREE NUDE GIRLS STANDING. Pencil. 570 mm×373 mm. Stamp of the artist's estate. Galerie Würthle, Vienna.

50 FEMALE NUDE STANDING BACK VIEW. Pencil. 554 mm by 368 mm. Stamp of the artist's estate. Albertina, Cat. No. 30,247.

51 FEMALE NUDE STANDING FRONT VIEW. Pencil. Signed. 564 mm×369 mm. Albertina, Cat. No. 23,530.

52 HALF-NUDE SITTING. Pencil, white chalk. 566 mm×370 mm. Stamp of the artist's estate. Dr. R. Leopold, Vienna.

53 GIRL'S HEAD FRONT VIEW. Pen and Indian ink, white chalk. 566 mm×369 mm. Stamp of the artist's estate. Albertina, Cat. No. 31,490.

54 LADY STANDING FACING RIGHT. Pencil. Signed. 496 mm by 324 mm. Albertina, Cat. No. 32,860.

55 GIRL IN LONG DRESS FACING LEFT. STUDY FOR AN UNCOMPLETED PORTRAIT. Pencil. 498 mm×322 mm. Albertina, Cat. No. 22,396.

PAINTINGS (COLOUR PLATES)

56 HYGIEIA. Detail from the picture "Medicine". Oil on canvas with gold. Signed. 430 cm×300 cm. Painted 1901. Final version 1907. Destroyed by fire 1945.

57 PORTRAIT OF EMILIE FLÖGE. Oil on canvas. Signed and dated 1902. 181 cm×84 cm. Historical Museum of the City of Vienna, Cat. No. 45,677.

58 PORTRAIT OF • GERTHA FELSÖVANYI. Detail. Oil on canvas. 150 cm×45,5 cm. In private possession, Vienna. Painted 1902.

59 WATER SERPENTS I. Tempera, water-colour on parchment with gold and silver. Signed. 50 cm×20 cm. Austrian Gallery, Vienna, Cat. No. 5077. Painted about 1904.

60 WATER SERPENTS II. Oil on canvas. Signed. 80 cm×145 cm. In private possession, Vienna. Painted 1904, revised 1907.

61 EXPECTATION. Working drawing for the Stoclet-frieze. Chalk, pencil, tempera, water-colour, opaque white, gold- and silver-bronze, gold- and silver-leaf on paper. 193,5 cm by 115 cm. Austrian Museum of Arts and Crafts, Cat. No. 37,197, Mal 226 E. Painted 1905 to 1909.

62 FULFILMENT. Working drawing for the Stoclet-frieze. Chalk, pencil, tempera, water-colour, opaque white, gold- and silver-bronze, gold- and silver-leaf on paper. 194,5 cm by 120,3 cm. Austrian Museum of Arts and Crafts, Cat. No. 37,197, Mal 226 A. Painted 1905 to 1909.

63 THE SUNFLOWER. Oil on canvas. Signed. 110 cm×110 cm. In private possession. Painted 1907.

64 PORTRAIT OF ADELE BLOCH-BAUER I. Detail. Oil on canvas with gold and silver. Signed and dated 1907. 138 cm×138 cm. Austrian Gallery, Vienna, Cat. No. 3830.

65 DANAE. Oil on canvas with gold. 77 cm×83 cm. In private possession, Graz. Painted 1907/08.

66 THE KISS. Oil on canvas with gold and silver. 180 cm by 180 cm. Austrian Gallery, Vienna, Cat. No. 912. Painted 1907/08.

67 THE BLACK FEATHER HAT. Oil on canvas. Signed and dated 1910. 79 cm×63 cm. In private possession, Graz.

68　ORCHARD WITH ROSES. Oil on canvas. Signed. 110 cm by 110 cm. In private possession, Lower Austria. Painted 1911 to 1912.

69　PORTRAIT OF ADELE BLOCH-BAUER II. Oil on canvas. Signed. 190 cm×120 cm. Austrian Gallery, Vienna, Cat. No. 4210. Painted 1912.

70　PORTRAIT OF THE BARONESS ELISABETH BACHOFEN-ECHT. Oil on canvas. Signed. 180 cm×128 cm. In private possession, Geneva. Painted about 1912.

71　THE MAIDEN. Oil on canvas. Signed. 190 cm×200 cm. Modern Gallery, Prague. Cat. No. 04,152. Painted 1913.

72　DEATH AND LIFE. Oil on canvas. Signed. 178 cm×198 cm. In private possession, Vienna. Painted before 1911, revised 1916.

73　THE WOMEN FRIENDS. Oil on canvas. Signed. 99 cm by 99 cm (?). Destroyed by fire 1945.

74　ADAM AND EVE. Chalk, oil on canvas. 173 cm×160 cm. Austrian Gallery, Vienna, Cat. No. 4402. Painted 1917/18. Unfinished.

75　THE BRIDE. Oil on canvas. 166 cm×190 cm. In private possession, Vienna. Painted 1917 to 1918. Unfinished.